NORTH WALES STEAM

STEAM

VOLUME TWO

E.N. Kneale

Frontispiece: The massive portals of Stevenson's Tubular Bridge and the old Castle make an imposing background to 'Britannia' class locomotive No. 70046 *Anzac* (but when this photograph was taken it was still unnamed) as it coasts down from Conwy in June 1957. On the left is the siding known as 'New York', used mainly for empty stock.

H. Rogers Jones

NORTH WALES STEAM

STEAM

VOLUME TWO

E.N.Kneale

Oxford Publishing Co.

An unidentified Class 2 tender locomotive heads a 'North Wales Land Cruise' back towards Rhyl in July 1954. The location is near Brynkir on the Caernarfon to Afon Wen branch line.

G. I. Davies

Dedication

To railwaymen, past and present

Typesetting by:
Aquarius Typesetting Services, New Milton, Hants.

Printed in Great Britain by:
Netherwood Dalton & Co., Huddersfield, Yorks.

Published by:
Oxford Publishing Co.
Link House
West Street
POOLE, Dorset.

Acknowledgements

British Railways (LMR)
Mr W. Jones
Mr R. V. Batchelor
Mr D. L. Williams
Mr W. Humphreys
Mr V. Bradley
Mrs Janet Owen
Mr I. Parry
Mr D. Fraser
Mr J. M. Lloyd
Mr G. Haulfryn Williams
Mr L. J. Davies
Mr E. Langford Lewis
Mr M. Catlin
Mr B. Vernon
Mr O. H. Parry
Mr B. Williams
Mr W. Edwards

Introduction

The purpose of this second volume, like the first, is to recall to mind some of the once familiar scenes that we enjoyed whilst travelling on the steam railway in North Wales.

In the first volume the emphasis was on the main Chester to Holyhead line. North Wales, however, had many other lines of which one was the busy Great Western line from Chester to Shrewsbury, passing through the large industrial tract around Wrexham.

In this volume, accordingly, attention, in part at least, is diverted to this eastern quarter, to which industry has but a distinction all of its own.

One hopes that in an age dominated by diesel and electric traction, the following plates will revive, with pleasant nostalgia, something of the majesty of steam. I must put on record my sincere gratitude to the friends and co-workers without whose help and expertise this volume would not have appeared. Three of them co-operated with me in forming the first book — Mr H. Rogers Jones, Mr B. A. Wynne and the late Mr H. A. Coulter. To their names I now hasten to add, with pleasure, those of Mr G. I. Davies and Mr K. Smith.

E. N. Kneale
Menai Bridge
Anglesey

Rhagair

Diben yr ail gyfrol yma, fel y cyntaf, yw dwyn i gof rhai o'r golygfeydd cyfarwydd yr arferem eu mwynhau wrth deithio ar y rheilffyrdd ager yng Ngogledd Cymru.

Yn y gyfrol gyntaf, 'roedd y pwyslais ar y brif reilffordd o Gaer i Gaergybi, ond 'roedd gan Ogledd Cymru nifer o gledrffyrdd eraill. Un ohonynt oedd lein brysur y 'Great Western' o Gaer i Amwythig a dramwyai dryw'r rhandir diwydiannol mawr sy'n amgylchynu Wrecsam.

O'r herwydd, yn y gyfrol hon trown ein sylw, yn rhannol o leiaf, at y chwarter Dwyreiniol yma sydd a naws unigryw i'w ddiwydiant. Gobeithiaf, mewn oes sy'n cael ei llywodraethu gan beiriannau disel a thrydan, y bydd y lluniau sy'n dilyn yn dwyn atgofion melys atoch o rywfaint o fawredd a gogoniant ager. Dyletswydd arnaf yw cofnodi fy niolchgarwch diffuant i'r cyfeillion a chydweithwyr a wnaeth ymddangosiad y gyfrol hon yn ddichonadwy drwy eu cymorth a'u harbenigrwydd. Bu tri ohonynt o gynorthwy imi gyda'r llyfr cyntaf — Mr H. Rogers Jones, Mr B. A. Wynne, a'r diweddar Mr H. A. Coulter. Hyfrydwch imi yw cael ychwanegu enwau Mr G. I. Davies a Mr K. Smith.

E. N. Kneale
Porthaethwy
Ynys Môn

Chester

The Great Western Shed

Plate 1: Pannier tank No. 8782 pushes an ex-Great Western Mogul, No. 5330, and an unidentified 'Hall' down the side of the shed at Chester in the early 1950s.

B. Flavell

Plate 2: Some of Chester's cleaners set to work on Great Western pannier tank engine, No. 1809, in the winter of 1928. It was not only main line locomotives that received this attention to cleanliness.

H. A. Coulter

Plate 3: In the summer of 1930, the fireman of Great Western 'Star' class locomotive No. 4061 *Glastonbury Abbey* uses a little of his muscle power to help turn his engine on Chester turntable.

H. A. Coulter

Plate 4: In July 1955, ex-Great Western Mogul No. 5375 awaits its turn of duty outside a shed that was thought to have been built on the site of the original LNWR engine shed. 'Hall' class locomotive No. 6926 *Holkham Hall* is seen close by.

G. I. Davies

Plate 5: Alongside the main shed, in August 1955, 'County' class locomotive No. 1022 *County of Northampton* passes slowly behind an ex-GWR Churchward 2-8-0 engine, No. 2810.

G. I. Davies

The LMS Shed

Plate 6: 'Black Five' No. 45130 runs slowly down the shallow gradient from Chester (Midland) Shed, and on to the main line between Crewe and Chester which will take her to Chester Station.
E. N. Kneale

Plate 7: On a fresh spring morning in 1962, rebuilt 'Jubilee' No. 45736 *Phoenix* moves slowly forward after having just been coaled on Chester Shed.
B. A. Wynne

Plate 8 (left): The lower quadrant signals on the over bridge in the centre of Chester Station, photographed in the summer of 1955. These signals were controlled from a small box just out of view and worked the crossovers in the middle of the station.

G. I. Davies

Plate 10 (above right): 'County' class locomotive No. 1008 *County of Cardigan* heads out of Chester Station on a warm summer's day in 1962 with a Birkenhead to Paddington express. The Hawksworth 'Counties' were handsome-looking engines, yet drivers and firemen had mixed feelings when asked about their performance.

E. N. Kneale

Plate 11 (below right): In August 1962, a parcels train waits patiently outside Chester Station. No. 1013 *County of Dorset* had brought in the train from Shrewsbury. The locomotive shed that can be seen in the background is the old Cheshire Lines shed at Chester (Northgate).

E. N. Kneale

Plate 9 (below): Despite the drizzle on an April day in 1962, No. 7015 *Carn Brea Castle* makes an attractive picture as she heads out of Chester Station with a train for Shrewsbury.

K. Smith

Awaiting Departure — Western Style

'Counties' at Chester

A Great Western Miscellany

Plate 12 (above): A sad day in the history of the through running of the Birkenhead to Paddington expresses in March 1967. Two 'Castle' class locomotives, Nos. 7029 *Clun Castle* and 4079 *Pendennis Castle* undertook to head the specials on that particular day. One of the 'Castles', No. 7029, is pictured travelling slowly along one side of the Chester triangle with four empty coaches, the occupants of which, with others, had earlier detrained and travelled on to Birkenhead behind a BR Class 5 locomotive.

E. N. Kneale

Plate 13 (left): A GWR unnamed 'Bulldog' class locomotive, No. 3335, backs down alongside Chester No. 4 box and under the LNWR lower quadrant signal gantry in the summer of 1929, prior to entering Chester Station.

H. A. Coulter

Plate 15 (above): What was eventually to become a common sight; a once proud locomotive bereft of name and numberplates, in this particular case No. 6833 *Calcott Grange*. She is seen accelerating away from Chester Station, in the summer of 1965, whilst in the background 'Black Five' No. 45300 waits on the centre road to also move off.

E. N. Kneale

Plate 14 (left): Ex-Great Western 0-6-0 No. 3208 performs shunting duties near No. 6 box, Chester in August 1962.

E. N. Kneale

The LMS at Chester

Plate 16: Preserved Stanier Pacific No. 46229 *Duchess of Hamilton* moves gently away from the platform at Chester, and with attendant coach proceeds on her journey to York, during the winter of 1983.

E. N. Kneale

Plate 17: Whilst backing down towards Chester Station, a 'Black Five' No. 44739, with Caprotti valve gear, passes alongside Chester No. 2 box, in the summer of 1955, and is overtaken by a Manchester to Llandudno train.

G. I. Davies

Plate 18: One of the Birkenhead-allocated Fairburn tank engines, No. 42086, takes on water from a very leaky water bag at the end of platform No. 3 on Chester Station in August 1966.

E. N. Kneale

Plate 19 (above): All the signs are here of the end of the steam era at Chester. One of the last Paddington to Birkenhead expresses has been brought in from Shrewsbury by 'Black Five' No. 44678. From the other end of the train can be seen a Stanier 2-6-4T locomotive, No. 42161, just about to bump up and couple itself to the coach and take the train on its last lap of its journey to Birkenhead (Woodside).

E. N. Kneale

Plate 20 (above right): On the centre road at Chester, a Hughes/Fowler 2-6-0 'Crab' comes to a stand at the head of a very long goods train during the summer of 1962.

E. N. Kneale

Plate 21 (below right): Ex-LMS Jubilee No. 45577 *Bengal* departs from Chester with a Birkenhead to Paddington express during the summer of 1964. In the final years 'Jubilees' and 'Black Fives' took over from the usual roster of ex-Great Western locomotives.

E. N. Kneale

BR Standards

Chester Triangle

Plate 22 (above left): Class 2 tank engine No. 84003 hurries its three coach train away from Chester and towards Wrexham in the summer of 1961. They will shortly enter Windmill Lane Tunnel — the first of two on the outskirts of Chester.

E. N. Kneale

Plate 23 (below left): BR Class 2 locomotive No. 78056 waits at the head of its two coach train at Chester in April 1962. The placing of the headlamp and the 6K shed plate suggests that it had probably worked in a local stopping train from Rhyl earlier in the day.

K. Smith

Plate 24 (above): A train from Birkenhead hauled by a Hughes/Fowler 2-6-0 'Crab' No. 42765, approaches the outer limits of the station in July 1962, whilst on the left of the picture 'Black Five' No. 45111 waits by the turntable.

E. N. Kneale

Plate 25 (below): 'Black Five' No. 44865 stands by the turntable in the summer of 1961, whilst in the background an unidentified 0-6-0 Class 4 locomotive is seen hauling a goods train, tender first, on the Cheshire Lines Railway. In all probability, they would be going to Northwich.

E. N. Kneale

Leaving Chester for the North Wales Coast

Plate 26: Passing Chester racecourse and leaving behind the familiar skyline of Chester, unnamed 'Patriot' No. 45551 picks up speed as it makes its way towards North Wales, in July 1961, with a Liverpool to Llandudno special.

K. Smith

Saltney   Junction for the GWR Line

Plate 27: An ex-Great Western 2-6-2T, No. 5179, having just crossed the River Dee during the winter of 1955, makes its way towards the yards at Saltney where she will spend most of the working day.

J. Peden

The Great Western Route to the South

Specials at Gresford Bank

Plate 28 (above left): 'Jubilee' class locomotive No. 45643 *Rodney* heads an 'up' Saturday special, near Saltney Junction, in July 1961.

K. Smith

Plate 29 (below left): Stanier Mogul No. 42950 heads a Llandudno to Manchester special through Saltney Cutting in July 1961. The lamps forming the headcode are different, to say the least.

K. Smith

Plate 30 (above): A most attractive picture of No. 7029 *Clun Castle* as she storms towards Gresford Bank which is caught by the sun's last rays on a March afternoon in 1967.

H. A. Coulter

Plate 31 (above): Preserved 'Jubilee' No. 5690 *Leander* blasts up Gresford Bank on a dull October morning in 1975.

E. N. Kneale

Plate 32 (right): On a typically misty November morning in 1969, one of Gresford Colliery's ex-Ministry of Supply 0-6-0s stands reflected in a large pool of water caused by heavy overnight rain.

E. N. Kneale

Gresford Colliery

Wrexham

Plate 33 (above): Wrexham on a warm summer's day in July 1962, sees 'Modified Hall' No. 6968 *Woodcock Hall* move away from the platform at the head of a Chester to Shrewsbury train. *Woodcock Hall* was, at this time, shedded at Westbury.

E. N. Kneale

Plate 34 (above right): Ex-GWR 0-4-2 No. 1458 comes to a stand in Wrexham (Central) Station with the 10.20a.m. train from Ellesmere, in June 1962.

K. Smith

Plate 35 (below right): 'Modified Hall' No. 7901 *Dodington Hall* rushes through Wrexham with a Paddington to Birkenhead express in August 1961.

E. N. Kneale

Freight Workings

Rhos Ddu Shed (Wrexham) — ex-GCR

Plate 36 (above left): During October 1965, 'Black Five' No. 45198 brings a train of mixed wagons slowly through Wrexham Station and on towards Shrewsbury.

E. N. Kneale

Plate 37 (below left): Ex-GWR 0-6-0PT No. 1628 brings its train of tankers through Wrexham Station in August 1961, whilst in the background, 'Manor' locomotive No. 7800 *Torquay Manor* crosses over to the 'down' fast line during a period of shunting stock.

E. N. Kneale

Plate 38 (above): All that remained of the Wrexham Great Central shed, Rhosddu, by the summer of 1963. When Chester's Great Western shed closed in 1960, some of their locomotives were moved to this shed.

E. N. Kneale

Plate 39 (below): Rhosddu Shed was eventually used as a store for either withdrawn engines, or those that were temporarily taken out of service.

E. N. Kneale

Brymbo

Croes Newydd Shed (Wrexham)

Plate 40 (above left): A Collett 0-6-2T, No. 6625, attacks the gradient up to Brymbo Steelworks with a train of iron-ore wagons in March 1964.

E. N. Kneale

Plate 41 (below left): Looking decidedly the worse for wear, 'Hall' class locomotive No. 5961 *Toynbee Hall* climbs away from Croes Newydd West Yard with its heavy train of iron-ore wagons in March 1964.

E. N. Kneale

Plate 42 (above): Standing by the coaling stage on the west side of Croes Newydd Shed, in the summer of 1964, are pannier tank No. 9610 and a Collett 0-6-2T, No. 6604.

E. N. Kneale

Plate 43 (above): Early morning sunlight casts long shadows as Great Western 2-6-2T No. 4555 is prepared for a Tal-y-Llyn special train, in September 1964, which she will eventually double-head with 'Manor' No. 7827 *Lydham Manor*.

E. N. Kneale

Plate 44 (below): First of the 'Manor' class, No. 7800 *Torquay Manor*, comes to rest outside the shed during the summer of 1962. She was shedded at Oswestry when this photograph was taken.

E. N. Kneale

Plate 45 (above right): Collett 0-6-2T No. 6651 approaches the shed whilst 0-6-0PT No. 3749 moves off towards the West Yard, at Croes Newydd in 1965.

E. N. Kneale

Plate 46 (below right): Shrewsbury's 'Jubilee' No. 45577 *Bengal* waits outside Croes Newydd Shed for her crew and her next turn of duty during the summer of 1964.

E. N. Kneale

The Roundhouse at Croes Newydd

Plate 47 (above): A Class 2 tender locomotive No. 46446 has just been turned on the turntable and reversed to her place in the roundhouse during the summer of 1965.

E. N. Kneale

Plate 48 (above right): Ex-GWR 0-6-2T No. 6602 had been withdrawn when this photograph was taken, and there was talk of preservation. She is seen being turned on Croes Newydd turntable.

E. N. Kneale

Plate 49 (below right): Ex-GWR 2-8-0 No. 3855 basks in the sunlight while its stable companions 0-6-0PT No. 9610 and 0-6-2T No. 6626 are left in the shadows, in July 1964.

E. N. Kneale

Plate 51 (above): BR Class 9, 2-10-0 No. 92125, is pictured about to leave the shed and work the heavy iron train up to Brymbo, during the summer of 1966. These engines took over from the ex-Great Western 2-8-0s and 0-6-2Ts as time went by.

E. N. Kneale

Plate 50 (left): 'Manor' class engine No. 7827 *Lydham Manor*, in immaculate condition, waits to leave the shed, where, in company with 2-6-2T No. 4555, it will run light engine to Ruabon and then will head the Tal-y-Llyn special to Towyn.

E. N. Kneale

Bersham Colliery

Plate 52 (left): Some of the fitters of Croes Newydd pose for the photographer beside 2-8-0 No. 3855 in July 1964.

E. N. Kneale

Plate 53 (right): Built by Hawthorne, Leslie & Co., one of Bersham Colliery's 0-4-0 saddle tanks, *Shakespeare*, clanks its way back to the shed.

E. N. Kneale

Plate 54 (below): 'Modified Hall' No. 7922 *Salford Hall* rushes past Bersham Colliery with a Shrewsbury to Chester train in July 1959.

K. Smith

Ruabon

Plate 55 (above): An ex-War Department 2-8-0, No. 90520, trundles its heavy load of permanent way materials through Ruabon in November 1964.

K. Smith

Plate 57 (right): 'County' Class 4-6-0 No. 1013 *County of Dorset* departs from Ruabon during the winter of 1958, heading a Shrewsbury to Chester train.

H. Rogers Jones

4-6-0 'Counties'

Plate 56 (above): Hawksworth 'County', No. 1011, *County of Chester* is seen running light engine south of Ruabon towards Shrewsbury in September 1964. The 'County' had brought in a Tal-y-Lyn special early in the day.

E. N. Kneale

Double-Headed Specials at Ruabon

Plate 58 (above): Two immaculate 'Dukedogs', Nos. 9017 and 9021 take over from Great Western 4-4-0 No. 3440 *City of Truro* at Ruabon, and continue their journey to Portmadoc in April 1958. No. 9017 was preserved and is now on the Bluebell line.

H. Rogers Jones

Plate 59 (above right): In September 1964, No. 7827 *Lydham Manor* and 2-6-2T No. 4555 double-head the Tal-y-Llyn special away from Ruabon and take the line to Llangollen, Bala and Barmouth Junction, and then to Towyn.

E. N. Kneale

Plate 60 (below right): The attractive-looking *City of Truro*, one of Churchwards 4-4-0 express engines, photographed in April 1958. It achieved fame in 1904 by being the first engine thought ever to exceed 100m.p.h. It is pictured being given the 'once over' by a tender full of school children!

H. Rogers Jones

Llangollen

Plate 61: BR Class 4 locomotive No. 75021 arrives at Llangollen Station with a train from Wrexham during March 1963.

E. N. Kneale

Plate 62: On a bright and crisp September morning, in 1963, BR Class 4 locomotive No. 75009 slips momentarily as she restarts her train from Berwyn Halt and heads towards Corwen and Bala.

E. N. Kneale

Berwyn

Corwen

Plate 63: The 'Royal Train', headed by two 'Manor' class locomotives, leave Corwen Station where they had made a stop to take on water. The two 'Manors' were No. 7819 *Hinton Manor* and No. 7822 *Foxcote Manor*, and they are seen making their way to Chester during August 1963.

E. N. Kneale

Plate 64: In November 1964, Ivatt 2-6-2T No. 41204, having arrived earlier with the 15.18 from Bala Junction, prepares to make its return journey from Bala at 16.05.

K. Smith

Bala

The LNWR Route into North Wales
Mold Junction

Plate 65: A fine study of a 'Grange' class locomotive, No. 6850 *Cleeve Grange* standing outside Mold Junction Shed.

B. A. Wynne

Plate 66 (above): 'Grange' class locomotive No. 6821 *Leaton Grange* moves slowly under the coaling tower at Mold Junction Shed to take on coal in March 1963.

E. N. Kneale

Coaling Up

Plate 67 (right): In March 1963, a coal wagon is hoisted to the top of the coaling tower where it will tip its contents of coal into the huge hopper, and then be lowered back again to rail level.

E. N. Kneale

Plate 68 (above): The shed master of Mold Junction Shed, J. E. Robinson, stands proudly beside rebuilt 'Royal Scot' No. 46115 *Scots Guardsman*. Mr Robinson's service with the railway extended to nearly forty years; his grandfather was Ben Robinson, the driver of *Hardwicke*, who made railway history with his epic run between Crewe and Carlisle in August 1895.

E. N. Kneale

Plate 70 (right): A Class N4 0-6-2T, No. 5920, takes on water near Shotton during winter 1930. This locomotive had once belonged to the Manchester, Sheffield and Lincolnshire Railway Company before being absorbed by the Great Central and then the LNER.

H. A. Coulter

Plate 69 (below): An ex-GWR 0-6-0PT hauls a mixture of wagons through Mold Junction Station in the winter of 1966. Mold Junction saw many types of ex-Great Western locomotives, but pannier tanks were, for some reason, rare.

E. N. Kneale

Shotton

Watering the Horse

Plate 73 (above): An ex-Midland 4F 0-6-0 No. 43981 waits outside Rhyl Shed. Note the heavy canvas weather or storm sheet on top of the cab roof.

B. A. Wynne

Plate 74 (below): In the summer of 1962, Class 2 tender engine No. 78031 moves slowly forward past the rear of Rhyl No. 2 box. Note the amount of signal ground rodding that was required to make the many movements.

B. A. Wynne

Plate 71 (above left): Ex-MS&LR 0-6-0 Pollitt saddle tank (LNER Class J62 No. 5883), built in 1897, and one of twelve, shunts at Connah's Quay. This locomotive was allocated to Bidston at the time until December 1936 after which it went on loan to Sir Robert McAlpine, together with Nos. 5885 and 5886, to assist in the construction of Ebbw Vale Steelworks.

H. A. Coulter

Plate 72 (below left): Ex-LNWR 'Claughton' class locomotive, No. 5947, hauls a 'down' North Wales Coast express near Mostyn during the summer of 1932.

H. A. Coulter

Plate 75: Fairburn 4MT 2-6-4T No. 42212 moves off the turntable on Rhyl Shed in October 1960.

B. A. Wynne

Plate 78 (right): A very popular summer attraction on the North Wales Coast was 'The Welsh Dragon', a shuttle service between the holiday resorts of Rhyl and Llandudno. Here, in August 1958, Ivatt 2-6-2T No. 41224, motor-fitted for push and pull working, emerges from Llanddulas Tunnel, near Old Colwyn, with its two coach train for Llandudno.

H. Rogers Jones

Plate 76: On a bright spring morning in April 1963, 'Jinty' No. 47350 is coaled in readiness for a day's work.

B. A. Wynne

Plate 77: 'Jubilee' class locomotive No. 45557 *New Brunswick* arrives at Rhyl Station at the head of a Holyhead to Crewe turn. This turn, or roster, was sometimes used for running ex-works engines, as in this particular instance in April 1960.

B. A. Wynne

Old Colwyn

Plate 79: On a warm summer's afternoon in August 1950, the driver of Ivatt 2-6-2T engine No. 41211, heading 'The Welsh Dragon', looks back down his two coach train to await the 'right away' from Old Colwyn Station.

A. Pratt

Colwyn Bay

Plate 80: One of Llandudno Junction's 'Black Fives', No. 45004, departs from Colwyn Bay Station, during the winter of 1964, with a train for Manchester.

E. N. Kneale

Plate 81 (above): The only locomotive of its kind built by British Railways. No. 71000 *Duke of Gloucester*, a three cylinder Caprotti valve gear Pacific, is pictured steaming past Colwyn Bay in January 1962, with the 'horse and carriage'.

E. N. Kneale

Mochdre & Pabo

Flying Scotsman

Plate 82 (left): After the naming ceremony of 'Patriot' No. 5525 *Colwyn Bay* at Colwyn Bay Station in the summer of 1937, some of the station staff and enginemen take the opportunity to have their photograph taken beside the engine.

Plate 83 (above): Preserved Pacific *Flying Scotsman* rushes past the small signal box of Mochdre & Pabo, between Colwyn Bay and Llandudno Junction, with The Gainsborough Model Railway Society special excursion from Doncaster to Llandudno in June 1966.

E. N. Kneale

The 'Up' 'Irish Mail'

Plate 84 (above): The unnamed 'Britannia', No. 70047, with an 'up' 'Irish Mail', gathers speed in September 1955 after the restriction of passing through Llandudno Junction Station.

H. Rogers Jones

Plate 85 (above right): Midland Compound No. 41167 arrives at Llandudno Junction with a train from Manchester in the early 1950s.

H. Rogers Jones

Plate 86 (below right): An unnamed 'Patriot', No. 45544, approaches Llandudno Junction with a summer excursion in June 1958.

H. Rogers Jones

Approaching Llandudno Junction
— from the East

Llandudno Junction

Plate 87 (above left): 'Jubilee' class locomotive No. 45612 *Jamaica*, heading a relief 'Irish Mail', overtakes BR Class 5 No. 73073 on a pick-up goods as they approach Llandudno Junction Station.

E. N. Kneale

Plate 88 (below left): Horwich-designed 2-6-0 'Crab' No. 42724 heads a returning excursion to Manchester from Llandudno, and is pictured on the 'up' slow line departing from Llandudno Junction, watched by some of the local railway enthusiasts.

H. Rogers Jones

Plate 89 (above): Rebuilt 'Scot' No. 46148 *The Manchester Regiment* (and pride of Llandudno Junction Shed) moves slowly away from Llandudno Junction Station, in February 1962, with a lightweight train of three coaches for Holyhead.

E. N. Kneale

'Royal Scots'

Plate 90: In May 1955, the morning Llandudno to London (Euston) train makes its departure from Llandudno Junction Station headed by rebuilt 'Scot' No. 46151 *Royal Horse Guardsman.*

H. Rogers Jones

Plate 91: Rebuilt 'Scot' No. 46117 *Welsh Guardsman* departs from Llandudno Junction for Euston, on a very cold February morning in 1958. The signal on the left of the picture was one of the tallest in North Wales, enabling it to be visible well beyond the station.

H. Rogers Jones

The Shed (6G)

Plate 92: An ex-LMS 0-6-0 4F, No. 44525, stands beneath the Llandudno Junction coaling tower in readiness for having its tender filled in January 1962.

E. N. Kneale

Plate 93: In October 1964, one of Croes Newydd's ex-Great Western locomotives, No. 6604, an 0-6-2T, makes a surprise appearance in Llandudno Junction Shed to make use of the wheel drop facilities. Attention was required to axleboxes and one big end bearing.

E. N. Kneale

Plate 94: The offending motion of No. 6604 awaits attention; the wheel drop can be seen in the foreground.

E. N. Kneale

Plate 95 (above): Sunday, outside Llandudno Junction Shed. The early morning sun highlights a couple of Stanier 3MT engines. No. 40130 was one of a batch built in 1935 with top feed and dome combined. Behind No. 40130 is a later version of the same type, but with top feed and separate dome. These locomotives were used very frequently on the Conwy Valley branch, which runs from Llandudno Junction to Blaenau Ffestiniog at a distance of 28 miles. In the background stands rebuilt 'Scot' No. 46157 *The Royal Artilleryman.*

H. Rogers Jones

Plate 96 (below): At Llandudno Junction, circa 1938, an ex-LNWR 0-6-2T, No. 7784, finds itself in what could only be called an embarrassing position. There's almost something tragi-comic about such happenings.

H. Rogers Jones

Eastern Region Invaders

Plate 97 (left): A Sunday afternoon in 1957 at Llandudno Junction Shed. 'Coronation' class engine No. 46248 *City of Leeds* glistens in the afternoon sunlight not many days after being out-shopped from Crewe Works.

H. Rogers Jones

Plate 98 (above): In August 1962, a Sheffield (Darnall) allocated 4-6-0 B1, No. 61004 *Oryx*, rests on Llandudno Junction Shed after having brought down a holiday special to Llandudno from the north of England.

E. N. Kneale

Plate 99 (below): In May 1964, LNER K4 2-6-0 No. 3442 *The Great Marquess* moves slowly off Llandudno Junction Shed after being serviced. The engine had worked a private charter party special from Leeds to Llandudno earlier in the day.

E. N. Kneale

Plate 100 (above): The beautiful light blue of a Caledonian Railway 4-2-2, No. 123, built in 1886. When in service with the LMS it was renumbered 14010 and was in red livery. She was withdrawn in 1935 and restored to original Caledonian colours as seen outside Llandudno Junction Shed in July 1953. She later proceeded to a 'Royal Journeys' exhibition at Llandudno Station and was attached to Queen Victoria's coach. Over 10,000 people paid to admire the train.

H. Rogers Jones

Plate 101 (below): In June 1937, the Liverpool and Manchester locomotive, *Lion*, trundles across the turntable with its train whilst, to the left of the picture, LMS streamlined locomotive No. 6220 *Coronation* is seen reversing towards the crossover at the Conwy end of the station. The other locomotive, but unfortunately not in the picture, was an ex-LNWR George V class locomotive, also named *Coronation*. These three locomotives had been brought together to form what would nowadays be called a public relations exercise. The four lines between Llandudno Junction and Colwyn Bay were closed to traffic for a couple of hours on a Sunday morning whilst the three locomotives and their trains ran almost side by side towards Colwyn Bay. The film cameramen used the 'up' slow line to take their moving and still shots.

H. Rogers Jones

On to Llandudno

Plate 102: A local passenger train, hauled by Class 2 tank engine No. 41235, departs from Llandudno Junction Station for Llandudno, in October 1960. The driver takes a quick backward glance down his three coach train as it crosses the main lines and takes the branch line to Llandudno. The signal box, footbridge and Maelgwyn Hotel have long since been demolished to make way for a flyover.

E. N. Kneale

Plate 103: A summer holiday special, hauled by an unidentified 'Black Five', runs alongside the Conwy estuary in August 1956, having just left Deganwy. Its next stop will be Llandudno.

H. Rogers Jones

Deganwy

Plate 104 (above): A Chester to Llandudno stopping train prepares to depart from Deganwy Station in October 1960. The Bangor-allocated 'Black Five' heading the train had just been outshopped from Crewe Works.

E. N. Kneale

Plate 105 (below): The 9.10a.m. Llandudno to London (Euston) train departs from Deganwy with 'Jubilee' class locomotive No, 45591 *Udaipur* at its head.

H. Rogers Jones

Plate 106: Steaming away from Glan Conwy Station with an afternoon train from Blaenau Ffestiniog in the summer of 1965, Fairburn tank engine No. 42074 runs alongside the River Conwy and will shortly join the main line at Llandudno Junction, where the train will terminate.

H. Rogers Jones

Plate 107: This part of the Llandudno Junction to Llandudno branch line always had a great deal of sand on the ballast, which had been swept in off the dunes close by. BR Class 4 No. 75010 passes beneath a modern looking bridge between Deganwy and Llandudno with a train from Chester in May 1958.

H. Rogers Jones

Llandudno

Plate 108 (above): All manner of locomotives were pressed into service during the very busy summer timetable in this part of North Wales. In the summer of 1960, a Fowler 0-6-0 4F is seen heading a special back to the Midlands. There is congestion at the terminus — Llandudno was often hectic acute, excursions from the north and Midlands arriving within minutes of each other. The signal box, turntable, water tower and most of the siding have now sadly disappeared.

H. Rogers Jones

Plate 110 (right): An ex-LNWR coal side tank, No. 7841, is pictured, in the early 1930s, near Llandudno carriage sidings with a local stopping train.

H. A. Coulter

Plate 109 (above): A Hughes/Fowler 2-6-0 'Crab', No. 13204, prepares to move off the Llandudno turntable after having taken on coal and water in the early 1930s.

H. A. Coulter

Plate 111 (above): On a late summer's afternoon in 1966, 'Jubilee' class locomotive No. 45660 *Rooke* slows down its train from Manchester as it approaches Llandudno Station.

B. A. Wynne

On to Conwy and Holyhead

Plate 112 (below left): A view captured in the summer of the late 1950s, from the last coach of a train departing from Llandudno Station. BR Class 4 2-6-0 No. 75010 accelerates briefly before shutting off steam as it reverses towards the station.

H. Rogers Jones

Plate 113 (above): Rebuilt 'Scot' No. 46120 *Royal Inniskilling Fusilier* tackles the 1 in 105 gradient leading up to the Conwy Tubular Bridge, after departing from Llandudno Junction Station with a stopping train to Holyhead in the summer of 1956.

H. Rogers Jones

Plate 114 (below): An unnamed Claughton hauls 'The Welshman' through Llandudno Junction in August 1930, whilst in the background a mixed traffic locomotive heads for Llandudno. 'The Welshman' used to run non-stop between Euston and Prestatyn, the next stop being Rhyl. Here the train would divide; the Criccieth, Pwllheli and Porthmadog portion then ran non-stop (as seen in this photograph) to Bangor. The engine came off there and usually one of the 4-6-2 tank engines of LNWR origin would take the train on to Afon Wen, where once again it would divide for the last time — the coaches going in opposite directions, some to Criccieth and Pwllheli and the others to Porthmadog. Whilst all this was happening, the remainder of 'The Welshman' carried on from Rhyl to Llandudno.

H. A. Coulter

Conwy

Rounding the Castle

Plate 115 (above): In June 1956, Stanier 2-6-4T No. 42588, with a local Bangor to Llandudno Junction train, leaves Conwy Station through the ancient town walls. The stone structures seen above the bunker were latrines for the soldiers guarding the 13th century castle walls.

H. Rogers Jones

Plate 116 (above right): A fine summer 1955 view of the 'up' 'Irish Mail' coasting round the tight curve (19-21 chains) through Conwy Station. The 'Britannia' class locomotive No. 70048 was later named *The Territorial Army 1908-1958* and was one of the first to be allocated to Holyhead mainly for 'Irish Mail' duties. Stevenson cleverly raised this part of the 13th century wall to form the archway over the line. An interesting feature is the signal post on the left of the picture; because of the extreme curvature of the line through Conwy Station, the 'up' signal has been sited on the 'down' signal post, so allowing the fireman of the engine to see the signal, as it were, across or through the bend.

H. Rogers Jones

Plate 117 (below right): A view not usually photographed because of the lighting conditions at this time of the day. It shows Conwy signal box, where most photographers chose to stand to take the much loved shot of trains coming through the arch in the town walls. Rebuilt 'Scot' No. 46165 *The Ranger (12th London Regiment)* heads a mid-morning Bangor to Chester express towards Llandudno Junction in the late spring of 1959.

H. Rogers Jones

Conwy to Penmaenmawr

Plate 118 (left): Ex-LMS 'Patriot' class locomotive No. 45503 *The Royal Leicester Regiment* attacks the incline leading out of Conwy Station and heads towards Penmaenmawr with a London to Holyhead express during the summer of 1956.
H. Rogers Jones

Plate 120 (right): This picture, made even more attractive by the rays of a setting sun, shows BR Class 4 locomotive No. 75031 making a spirited departure from Penmaenmawr with a train for Chester.
H. Rogers Jones

Plate 121 (below right): Always an attraction, even to holiday-makers, was the 'up' 'Irish Mail', seen passing Penmaenmawr in August 1954 headed by rebuilt 'Royal Scot' No. 46118 *Royal Welsh Fusilier.*
G. I. Davies

Plate 119 (below): 'Royal Scot' No. 6113 *Cameronian* sweeps round the curve at Morfa Bycham, between Penmaenmawr and Conwy, heading a Holyhead to London (Euston) express.
H. A. Coulter

Aber

Plate 122 (above): 'Royal Scot' No. 6120 *Royal Inniskilling Fusilier* heads a Bangor to London (Euston) express near Aber in the autumn of 1935.

H. A. Coulter

Plate 124 (right): In the early 1930s, an ex-LNWR 'George V' class locomotive, No. 5406 *Llandrindod* double heads with a Midland Compound. They are pictured between Llanfairfechan and Aber with an express for Holyhead.

H. A. Coulter

Plate 123 (above): On a warm summer afternoon in August 1954, 'Black Five' No. 44874, running tender first with a stopping train for Llandudno, passes the small signal box and prepares to stop at Aber Station.

G. I. Davies

Tal-y-bont

Plate 125 (above): An ex-LNWR 'Experiment' class 4-6-0 heads a very long train of cattle wagons away from Bangor Tunnel and on towards Aber, during the summer of 1935.

H. A. Coulter

Plate 127 (right): Midland Compound No. 1067, picking up speed after leaving Colwyn Bay, heads a Manchester to Llandudno train towards Mochdre on a summer afternoon in 1937.

H. A. Coulter

Plate 126 (above): In the early 1930s, an ex-LNWR 2-cylinder 0-8-0 hauls a heavy load of mixed freight on to the viaduct at Tal-y-Bont with a Menai Bridge to Mold Junction goods train.

H. A. Coulter

Plate 128 (above): An impressive sight as 'Royal Scot' No. 6162 *Queen's Westminster Rifleman* heads a 'down' 'Irish Mail' near the village of Tal-y-Bont in the mid-1930s.

H. A. Coulter

Llandegai

Plate 129 (left): 'Royal Scot' No. 6118 *Royal Welsh Fusilier* sweeps round the curve near Llandegai and heads towards Bangor with a London to Holyhead express, in the early 1930s.

H. A. Coulter

Penryhn Sidings

Plate 130: An unusual but pleasing combination of an ex-LNWR coal side tank and a 'Prince of Wales' class tank engine. They are seen not far from Penrhyn Sidings, in the early 1930s, with a four-coach local train for Llandudno.

H. A. Coulter

Bethesda Junction

A Miscellany of Motive Power

Plate 131 (above): Bursting into the sunlight from the darkness of Bangor Tunnel, during the summer of 1931, 'Royal Scot' No. 6162 rapidly picks up speed after having left Bangor Station not many minutes before. Unnamed at this particular time, it was eventually named *Queen's Westminster Rifelman.*

H. A. Coulter

Plate 133 (right): This view, photographed from Bethesda Junction signal box, in August 1954, shows Stanier 8F No. 48292 running light engine past the signal box and on towards Llandudno Junction.

G. I. Davies

Plate 132 (above): An August 1954 view, photographed from near the top of Bangor Tunnel, showing the Bethesda branch line heading off to the right. 'Black Five' No. 45028 is seen bringing in a local train towards the crossing. Prior to World War II, the Bethesda branch was extremely busy, and during weekdays there were seven passenger trains in the morning and seven during the afternoon and evening, and also one goods train. A time of fifteen minutes was given for this turn between Bangor and Bethesda, a distance of a little over five miles, stopping at Felin Hen Halt and Tregarth, and the return fare was 6d. (2½p.). Every Saturday night, eleven return trips were made, starting with the 5.22p.m. from Bangor. It must be remembered that Bethesda and district had a population of around 7,000 of which nearly 2,000 worked in the Penryhn Quarry; hence the reason for so many daily trains to and from Bangor.

G. I. Davies

Plate 134 (above): Ex-War Department 2-8-0 No. 90650 works an 'up' freight out of Bangor Tunnel in August 1954. Over nine hundred of these locomotives were built during the war years, and after the 'D' Day landings quite a number of them saw service on the Continent.

G. I. Davies

Plate 135 (below): In August 1954, the 'North Wales Land Cruise' train, on its return journey from Barmouth, rushes out of Bangor Tunnel and past Bethesda Junction box, headed by an unidentified BR Class 2 tender locomotive.

G. I. Davies

Bangor

Plate 136: On a bright frosty morning, in January 1965, and after a light overnight fall of snow, BR Class 4 No. 75009 slips briefly as it completes a shunting movement on the 'down' relief line in Bangor Station.

E. N. Kneale

Plate 139: Storming away from Bangor in the summer of 1963, after having had a signal check, 4-6-2 Pacific No. 46251 *City of Nottingham* passes Bangor No. 2 box and heads for Holyhead with an express from London.

E. N. Kneale

Plate 137 (above left): The imposing lines of a Stanier 'Coronation' class locomotive are clearly seen in this view of No. 46225 *Duchess of Gloucester* as she prepares to depart from Bangor Station with a Holyhead to Crewe train in April 1963. In 1955, this particular engine produced the highest continuous steaming rate for any passenger locomotive in the United Kingdom whilst in the test plant at Rugby.

E. N. Kneale

Plate 140 (below): In the summer of 1960, an Edge Hill-allocated 'Princess Royal' class locomotive pays a welcome visit to North Wales. 'Princess Royals' were not that common and, in most instances, were on running in turns from Crewe Works. No. 46204 *Princess Louise* was later to head a Holyhead to Crewe train.

B. A. Wynne

Plate 138 (left): On a warm summer evening in 1964, No. 46237 *City of Bristol* simmers gently at the head of a postal train bound for Crewe. An interesting feature is the Egyptian style of architecture for the tunnel entrance. The signal gantry had to be placed this low so that the locomotive crews could sight the signals as they were approached from within the tunnel. In 1956, this locomotive was loaned to the Western Region for trials with a 'King' class engine that had had superheater modifications, and was also fitted with double blastpipe and chimney. Both the 4-6-2 and the 4-6-0 locomotives acquitted themselves well.

E. N. Kneale

Plate 141 (above): On 21st August 1966, The Altrincham Railway Excursion Society ran a Holyhead and Brymbo special, headed by ex-LNER A2 Pacific No. 60532 *Blue Peter*. Originally the train was to have been hauled by an A4. The A2 is pictured running through Bangor Station on the 'down' fast line, watched by a solitary enthusiast.

E. N. Kneale

Plate 142 (above right): Relegated to the mundane working of a parcels train (The Horse & Carriage), in March 1964, No. 46256 *Sir William Stanier* moves slowly away from Bangor and on towards Llandudno Junction.

B. A. Wynne

Plate 143 (right): 'Britannia' class locomotive No. 70054 *Dornoch Firth* moves slowly out of the shadows of Bangor Shed accompanied by 2-6-2T No. 41233 during the autumn of 1964. They were both to come back on shed, but on to a different road.

E. N. Kneale

Pre-Nationalisation

Plate 144 (above): 'Royal Scot' No. 6163, unnamed in this photograph, but later to become *Civil Service Rifleman*, departs from Bangor with a train for Chester in the early 1930s.
H. A. Coulter

Plate 145 (above right): An 'up' relief 'Irish Mail' thunders through Bangor Station in the summer of 1963 headed by 'Black Five' No. 45324. The 2-6-2T in the background is No. 41200; it is standing in what used to be the Bethesda bay.
E. N. Kneale

Plate 146 (right): In the early 1930s, 'Prince of Wales' class ex-LNWR 4-6-0 No. 5762 enters Bangor Station on a warm summer day with a train for Chester.
H. A. Coulter

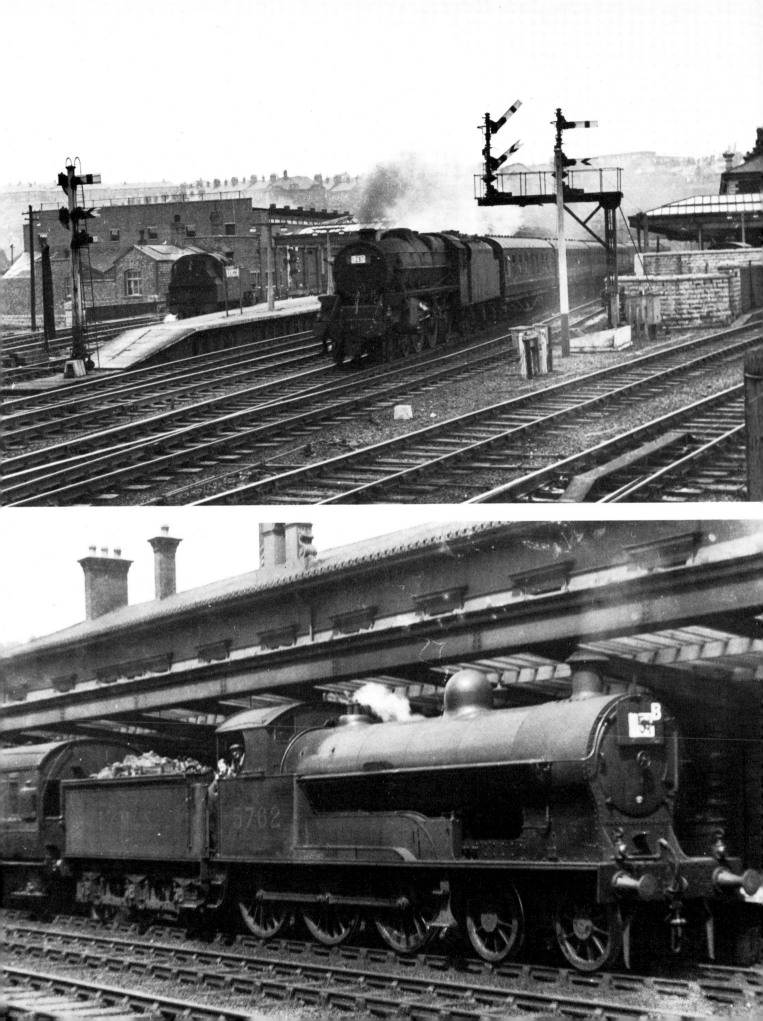

Freight Workings

Plate 147 (above): Ex-LMS 0-6-0 4F hauls its heavy load of mixed wagons past No. 2 box and through Bangor Station with a Menai Bridge to Mold Junction goods in March 1963.

E. N. Kneale

Plate 149 (right): A wet and miserable day in January 1965, somehow fitting for such a sad occasion. 'Black Five' No. 45111 hauls two dead engines on the first part of their journey to the scrapyard at Morriston in South Wales. One is rebuilt 'Royal Scot' No. 46148 *The Manchester Regiment*, once the pride of Llandudno Junction Shed, but in its last days was shedded at Holyhead, followed by the last of Bangor's 4Fs, No. 44478.

B. A. Wynne

Plate 148 (right): In January 1963, ex-LNWR 0-8-0 No. 48895 moves off Bangor Shed and passes No. 2 box on its way to Menai Bridge goods yard to eventually work the evening goods to Mold Junction. This locomotive had, prior to its rebuilding, been a 2-8-0 Compound.

B. A. Wynne

Plate 150: Driver and fireman prepare 'Black Five' No. 44808 on Bangor Shed for a late evening turn during the winter of 1964.

E. N. Kneale

Plate 151: A grand old lady; the ex-LNWR coal side tank engine preserved through the efforts of Bangor's one-time shed master, Mr. J. Dunn. It is pictured on the day prior to its departure to Penryhn Castle Museum in March 1964. The locomotive's chimney was removed, as it was too high to go under the gateway leading to the castle.

E. N. Kneale

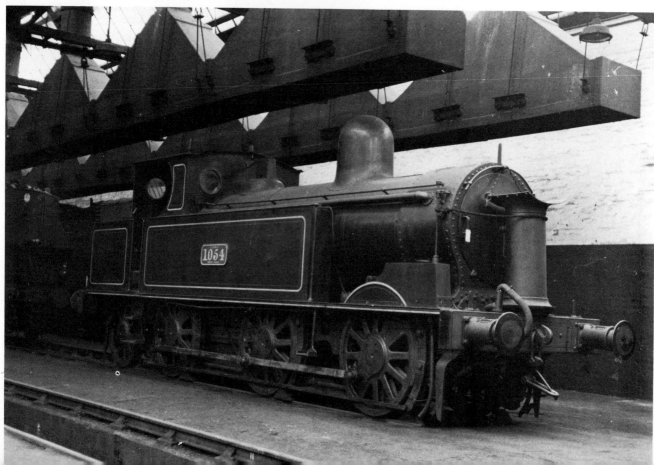

Plate 152: A typical Sunday morning scene outside Bangor Shed during the summer of 1963. The locomotives on view are Nos. 45324, 42198, 78058, 45247, 41200, 42489, 42446, 42282 and 78003 and, out of shot and within the shed, possibly another fifteen or twenty.

B. A. Wynne

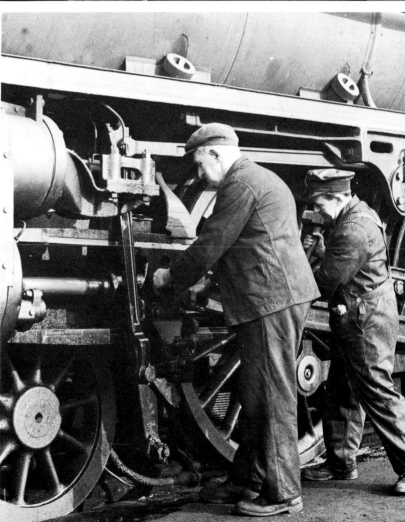

Plate 153: A fitter and his mate tighten up a cross-head nut on 'Black Five' No. 45223 during the summer of 1963.

B. A. Wynne

Menai Bridge

Light Engines

Plate 156 (above): The signalman in Menai Bridge box leans out of the window to watch Bangor's two Royal 'Black Fives', Nos. 45247 and 45282 make their way towards Caernarfon. The occasion was the visit of Her Majesty the Queen to North Wales in August 1963. Type 4 diesel No. D308 hauled the Royal train from London (Euston) to Caernarfon. The two 'Black Fives' then took over from No. D308 and worked the train as far as Afon Wen, where ex-GWR locomotives were waiting to take the Royal train on to Criccieth. The Queen's ultimate destination on this visit to Wales was Aberystwyth.   *E. N. Kneale*

Plate 154 (left): The Amlwch pull and push train, with 2-6-2T No. 41267 at its head, hurries away from Menai Bridge Station on a late summer evening in 1962, the next stop being Bangor. In the background, coming down the Caernarfon branch tender first, is one of Bangor's Class 2 tender engines.

E. N. Kneale

Plate 155 (below left): In the summer of 1963, the early morning peace of a small country station is shattered by the exhaust of a Class 2 tank engine slipping on damp rails. The first Amlwch pull and push train of the day departs from Menai Bridge Station; its next stop will be in Anglesey at Llanfair P.G.

E. N. Kneale

Plate 157 (below): Three locomotives rush through Menai Bridge Station early on a Saturday morning in the summer of 1962, and proceed up the Caernarfon branch. One of these engines will come off at Caernarfon and the Bangor men will work the first train out of the town as far as Llandudno Junction. The other two engines will carry on to Afon Wen, where they will pick up empty carriages and take them to Pen-y-Chain, a station close to Butlin's Holiday Camp, where, after running round their train, they will make for Bangor with a full load of holiday-makers returning home. The three locomotives are Nos. 42075, 42947 and 41200.

E. N. Kneale

'Britannia' Pacifics at Work

The Caernarfon Line

Plate 158 (above left): An express for Holyhead approaches Menai Bridge Station headed by No. 70024 *Vulcan* during the summer of 1963. When newly built, this engine entered service on the Western Region, being first allocated to Plymouth (Laira), then to Cardiff (Canton), before eventually being allocated to the Midland Region.

E. N. Kneale

Plate 159 (left): 'Britannia' class locomotive No. 70046 *Anzac*, with more than enough steam to spare, passes Menai Bridge box with an 'up' 'Irish Mail'. The engine had lost its nearside nameplate, but not the offside one, when this photograph was taken in the summer of 1962.

E. N. Kneale

Plate 160 (above): A Bangor to Pwllheli train, headed by Fairburn tank No. 42283, comes off the main Chester to Holyhead line at Menai Bridge in the summer of 1963, and, after stopping at the station, will tackle a short but stiff climb up to Treborth Station, which was closed in March 1959, and so on to Caernarfon.

E. N. Kneale

Plate 163 (above): Having been brought to a stand at the Menai Bridge outer home signal during the summer of 1963, Stanier 2-6-4T No. 42482 moves off down the incline to Menai Bridge Station. The main Chester to Holyhead line is in the foreground.

E. N. Kneale

Plate 161 (above left): Two Fairburn tank engines, Nos. 42075 and 42212, double-head a very lightweight train from Pwllheli to Bangor during the summer of 1962. They are seen crossing over from the branch line to the main line at Menai Bridge.

E. N. Kneale

Treborth Bank

Plate 162 (left): In the summer of 1963, Stanier 2-6-4T No. 42478 climbs Treborth bank on its way to Caernarfon and Pwllheli. Menai Bridge goods yard is on the left, and on the extreme left of the picture part of the Menai Suspension Bridge can be seen.

E. N. Kneale

Plate 164 (right): High summer on the Caernarfon branch in 1962. A Fairburn tank engine, No. 42209, brings her train under Treborth bridge and down the bank to the main line with a Butlin's special, full of holiday-makers returning home, from Pen-y-Chain to Chester.

E. N. Kneale

Port Siding

Caernarfon

Plate 166: BR Class 4 locomotive No. 75027 with blower on and safety-valves lifting, waits to depart from Caernarfon Station with a special for Chester.

E. N. Kneale

Station Staff

Plate 167 (right): The stationmaster at Caernarfon, and his staff, pose for the camera during the summer of 1962.

E. N. Kneale

Plate 165 (left): The singling of branch lines usually heralded their eventual closure, and the Menai Bridge to Caernarfon line was no exception. 'Black Five' No. 45298, with a train of sleepers from Caernarfon goods yard, passes the very tall Port Siding signal box, near Port Dinorwic, in the summer of 1966.

E. N. Kneale

Freight Workings

Plate 168 (above): A mixed goods train draws slowly away from Caernarfon on a misty April morning in 1965, hauled by Fairburn tank engine No. 42283. The train will eventually make its way down the branch to Menai Bridge Station and then set back into the goods yard.

E. N. Kneale

Plate 169 (above right): Fairburn 2-6-4T No. 42283 shunts Caernarfon goods yard in April 1965.

E. N. Kneale

Plate 170 (right): In the summer of 1965, 'Black Five' No. 45298 makes up her train of mostly empty cattle wagons whose eventual destination will be Holyhead, whilst BR Class 4 No. 75009 will, after some shunting, run up the Llanberis line and shunt at Pontrhythallt.

E. N. Kneale

Plate 171: On a bright winter morning in 1963, BR Class 2 tender engine No. 78059 departs from Caernarfon Station, after having spent most of the morning there working the yard.

B. A. Wynne

Plate 172 (below): In October 1962, 'Princess Royal' class No. 46203 *Princess Margaret Rose* was withdrawn and placed in store at Carlisle (Kingmoor) depot. Shortly after, she was purchased by Sir Billy Butlin who had her beautifully restored at Crewe Works to original LMS condition. She is seen here shortly after arriving at Caernarfon Station on her way to her new home in May 1963.

E. N. Kneale

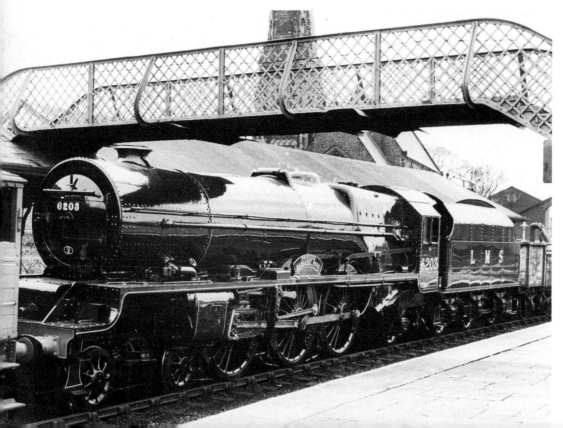

Plate 173 (above right): Having taken on water, Ivatt Class 4 No. 43052 departs from Caernarfon Station, in May 1963, with its treasured charge on the final leg of its journey from Crewe to Butlin's Holiday Camp, near Pwllheli.

E. N. Kneale

Plate 174 (right): A summer 1962 late evening Bangor to Pwllheli local train, having just passed Waterlooport, now approaches No. 1 box and then Caernarfon Station, hauled by Fairburn 2-6-4T No. 42076.

E. N. Kneale

Semaphores

Pontrhythallt

The Llanberis Branch

Plate 175: On a bitterly cold morning, in the winter of 1965/6, 'Black Five' No. 44711 shunts empty wagons at Pontrhythallt on the Llanberis branch.

E. N. Kneale

Plate 176: A BR Class 4 locomotive, No. 75009, prepares to run light engine back to Caernarfon in the summer of 1965. The guard can be seen coupling up the guard's van to the engine at Pontrhythallt.

E. N. Kneale

Llanberis

Plate 177: Running tender first towards Llanberis Station, BR Class 4 No. 75029 will shunt empty wagons ready for the demolition gang to commence lifting the track during the winter of 1965/6.

E. N. Kneale

Britannia Tubular Bridge

Plate 180 (above): This was always a lovely place to sit and watch the trains go by. You were never quite sure what would come bursting out of the 'up' tube, unless you had heard the engine whistle before entering the tube on the Anglesey side, but that didn't always happen. 'Black Five' No. 44860 is seen, in the summer of 1962, coming out of the 'up' tube into the warmth of a summer afternoon. Would that we could witness this scene again; alas, never.

E. N. Kneale

Plate 178 (above left): 'Black Five' No. 45311 heads a train of empty cattle wagons past Menai Bridge goods yard during the winter of 1962. Part of the Menai Suspension Bridge can be seen in the background.

B. A. Wynne

Plate 179 (left): An unnamed 'Claughton', No. 5928, rushes through Menai Woods with the first part of 'The Welshman' in the early 1930s.

H. A. Coulter

Plate 181 (right): So now you know!

E. N. Kneale

LONDON AND NORTH WESTERN RAILWAY CAUTION

PERSONS TRESPASSING UPON THE RAILWAYS BELONGING TO, OR LEASED OR WORKED BY, THE LONDON AND NORTH WESTERN RAILWAY COMPANY, OR BY THAT COMPANY AND ANY OTHER COMPANY, AND ANY PERSONS TRESPASSING UPON THE STATIONS CONNECTED WITH SUCH RAILWAYS, ARE LIABLE TO A PENALTY OF FORTY SHILLINGS, UNDER THE LONDON AND NORTH WESTERN RAILWAY ADDITIONAL POWERS ACT, 1883, AND, IN ACCORDANCE WITH THE PROVISIONS OF THE SAID ACT, PUBLIC WARNING IS HEREBY GIVEN TO ALL PERSONS NOT TO TRESPASS UPON THE SAID RAILWAYS OR STATIONS.

Euston Station London
December 1883

BY ORDER

RHYBUDD

MAE PERSONAU DRESPASONT AR REILFFYRDD YN CAEL EU PERCHENOGI NEU EU PRYDLESU GAN GWMPEINI Y LONDON & NORTH WESTERN RAILWAY, NEU YN CAEL EU GWEITHIO GANDDYNT, NEU GANDDYNT HWY AC UNRHYW GWMPEINI ARALL AC HEFYD UNRHYW BERSONAU DRESPASONT AR ORSAFOEDD Y CYFRYW REILFFYRDD YN AGORED I DDIRWY O DDEUGAIN SWLLT, O DAN Y LONDON & NORTH WESTERN RAILWAY, ADDITIONAL POWERS ACT, 1883, AC YN UNOL A THELERAU YR ACT DYWEDEDIG RHODDIR TRWY HYN I BAWB RYBUDD CYHOEDDUS I BEIDIO TRESPASU AR Y RHEILFFYRDD NAC AR Y GORSAFOEDD DYWEDEDIG.

GORSAF EUSTON LLUNDAIN
RHAGFYR, 1883.

TRWY ORCHYMYN

ERECTED ANNO DOMINI
ROBERT STEPHENSON ENGINEER

'Blue Peter'

Plate 184 (above): The A2 ex-LNER Pacific, No. 60532 *Blue Peter*, on its homeward journey from Holyhead to Manchester, crosses from the island of Anglesey to the mainland, via Stephenson's Tubular Bridge, in August 1966.

D. East

Plate 182 (above left): A Manchester to Holyhead express, hauled by 'Black Five' No. 45091, rushes into the 'down' tube and across the Menai Straits, and so on to Anglesey during the summer of 1960.

E. N. Kneale

Plate 183 (left): In the summer of 1962, a setting sun causes long shadows to be cast by the coaches of the last pull and push train of the day to Amlwch, as it enters the 'down' tube of the Britannia Bridge — next stop Llanfair P. G.

E. N. Kneale

Llanfair P.G.

Plate 185: BR Class 4 No. 75009 runs tender first through Llanfair P. G. Station with chemical tanks from Amlwch, during the summer of 1965. The name of the station in full can be seen above the rose bushes.

E. N. Kneale

Gaerwen   Junction for Amlwch

Plate 186: Whilst waiting for the next main line train to stop at Gaerwen in the summer of 1964, and one which will connect with the Amlwch pull and push, the driver and fireman are deciding between themselves whether to have their tea in the compartment of one of the carriages, or to walk over to No. 2 box and have it with the signalman.

E. N. Kneale

Plate 187 (above): A summer 1961 view of Gaerwen, as seen from the Amlwch branch, showing Gaerwen Station and Gaerwen No. 2 box. On the main line, rebuilt 'Royal Scot' No. 46150 *The Life Guardsman* heads a Holyhead to Manchester express towards the station.

E. N. Kneale

Plate 188 (right): A Mold Junction 2-8-0 provides an unusual source of power for a Chester to Holyhead parcels train, seen passing through Gaerwen Station in the winter of 1964/5.

E. N. Kneale

Plate 189 (below): The Amlwch pull and push train waits patiently in a siding near No. 2 box at Gaerwen in the summer of 1964. Only after the main line train has arrived and departed will the two-coach train move out of the siding and cross over to the 'down' platform to take on passengers for all stations to Amlwch.

E. N. Kneale

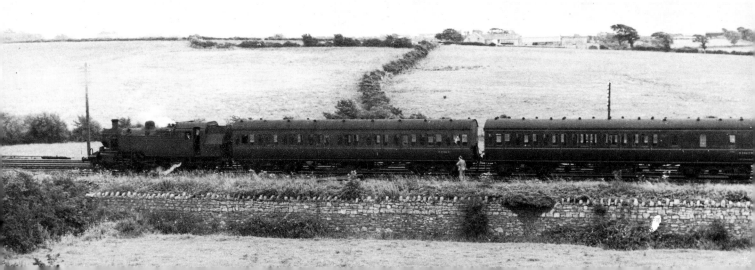

The Amlwch Branch

Llangefni

Plate 190: Engine and van steam away from Llangefni Station and make their way to Amlwch, on a February morning in 1964. The engine is a Stanier 2-6-4T, No. 42478.

E. N. Kneale

Amlwch

Plate 191: The fireman of BR Class 2 tank engine No. 84003 heaves down on the water tower chain so allowing water to flow into the engine's tanks. The driver seems to be in a thoughtful mood in this scene, photographed at Amlwch in the summer of 1964.

E. N. Kneale

Plate 192: A BR Class 4 locomotive, No. 75009, arrives at the Associated Octel yard at Amlwch, and prepares to make up its train of chemical tanks for the return journey to Llandudno Junction, during the winter of 1966.

E. N. Kneale

Bodorgan

Pre-Nationalisation Days

Plate 193: 'Royal Scot' No. 6161 *King's Own* hurtles past the small country station of Bodorgan with an 'up' 'Irish Mail' during the summer of 1935.

H. A. Coulter

Plate 194: 'Britannia' class Pacific No. 70001 *Lord Hurcomb* was first shedded at Stratford and then at March before being reallocated to Willesden, when this photograph was taken in the summer of 1963. The engine is pictured resting on Holyhead Shed after having brought in a relief express.

B. A. Wynne

Plate 197: In the winter of 1963, an ex-Cardiff (Canton) 'Britannia', No. 70027 *Rising Star*, rests inside Holyhead Shed. Western Region 'Britannias' were quite rare in North Wales, and it was only when many of them had been reallocated to the Midland Region, particularly to Aston, in the Midlands, that they began to appear a little more often.

E. N. Kneale

Plate 198 (right): The shed master of Holyhead, Mr Lomax, a well-liked and much-respected gentleman both by his staff and by visiting railway enthusiasts, is pictured in his office during the spring of 1963.

E. N. Kneale

Plate 195 (above left): Holyhead Shed, as seen on a winter afternoon in 1962. The locomotives on view are, from left to right, rebuilt 'Royal Scot' No. 46150 *The Life Guardsman*, No. 46225 *Duchess of Gloucester*, No. 70016 *Ariel* and 'Black Five' No. 45180.

E. N. Kneale

Plate 196 (left): No. 70012 *John of Gaunt* draws out of the shed two 'Black Fives', Nos. 45145 and 45237, during the spring of 1964. The other 'Britannia' Pacific is No. 70045 *Lord Rowallan* and the 'Black Five' is No. 45045.

E. N. Kneale

Plate 199: During the winter of 1962, Stanier Pacific No. 46225 *Duchess of Gloucester* moves slowly off Holyhead Shed, whilst on the left is rebuilt 'Royal Scot' No. 46150 *The Life Guardsman* and to the right No. 70016 *Ariel*.

E. N. Kneale

Plate 200: The foreman's assistant at Holyhead in the 1960s was Mr Billington, seen here checking the roster lists.

E. N. Kneale

The End of the Line

Plate 201: Making a painfully slow but successful departure from Holyhead Station with a heavy train, 'Royal Scot' No. 6126 *Sanspareil* throws up a pall of smoke and steam as she slips briefly, but violently, on her way up the steep gradient in the early 1930s. In the background, near the coaling stage, an ex-LNWR Ramsbottom 0-6-0 saddle tank rests between shunting duties. No. 6126 was later to lose her name *Sanspareil* and was renamed *Royal Army Service Corps*.

H. A. Coulter

Plate 202: The Holyhead 'Jintys' were, as in many other places, 'maids of all work'. Some of the prodigious loads that these small tank engines hauled up the Holyhead Bank had to be seen to be believed. During the winter of 1964, ex-LMS 0-6-0 3F No. 47410 hauls its heavy load very slowly up the incline — and without so much as a hint of a slip.

E. N. Kneale

Plate 203: Rebuilt 'Royal Scot' No. 46155 *The Lancer* makes its departure from Holyhead Station with an 'up' relief 'Irish Mail' in the summer of 1964. For years the 'Scots' reigned supreme at Holyhead, and mastered the heaviest of trains, but the introduction of the English Electric Type 4 diesels unfortunately saw them rapidly become relegated to the reliefs, and then, of course, they faded away and 'Black Fives' took over. This was possibly the last time a 'Royal Scot' worked a relief 'Irish Mail' out of Holyhead.

E. N. Kneale

×15